The Basics

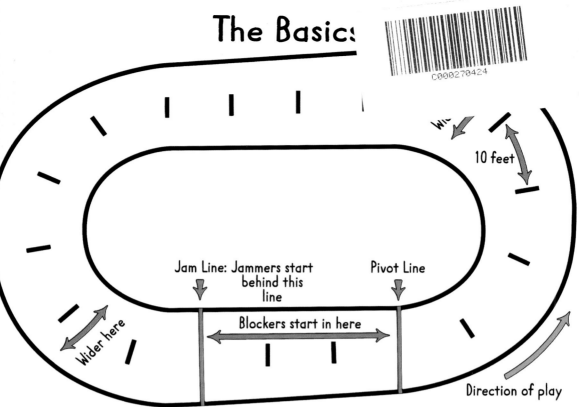

Jam Line: Jammers start behind this line

Pivot Line

Blockers start in here

Wider here

10 feet

Wider here

Direction of play

Flat Track Roller Derby is played on an oval track, slightly wider on the apex. Players must be deemed ready to play safely by their league before they can participate in games or scrimmages. They used to have to pass "minimum skills" which included being able to skate 27 laps in 5 minutes!

It's a full contact sport played on skates. Each team has 4 blockers and 1 jammer on track at once. The jammer, the skater with a star on their helmet, must pass the other team's blockers' hips, after an initial lap in order to score.

The Players

Jammer

How to spot them:	They have a star on their helmet cover.
How many per jam:	One per team on track at time.
Special ability:	Only one who can score points.
Special rules:	Has to get past other team's blockers to score.
	Must start behind jam line.
	Cannot score if their star helmet cover isn't on.
	The first jammer who passes all opposing players becomes "lead jammer" and gains the ability to end the jam.

Blocker

How to spot them:	They have no helmet cover.
How many per jam:	From 1 to 4 blockers per team on track at a time.
Special ability:	They stop the other team's jammer from scoring.
	They can help their own jammer score.
Special rules:	Must start between the jam line and pivot line.
	One must be on track for the game to proceed.

The Pivot

How to spot them:	They have a stripe on their helmet cover.
How many per jam:	Up to one per team on track.
Special ability:	They are a blocker that can start on the pivot line. They can receive the star helmet cover from the jammer and become the jammer.
Special rules:	They are not essential. The game can proceed without a blocker being designated as a pivot.

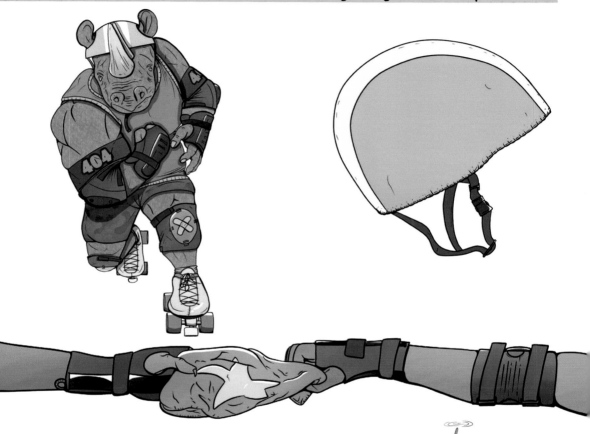

The Team:

Each team can have a roster of up to 15 players.

They also have coaches and other team staff there to help them. You can spot them easily as they will not be wearing skates or protective gear and are generally near their team's bench. The bench staff can have a variety of roles from helping with strategy to maintaining the wellbeing of players.

The Referees/Refs

There are up to 8 referees in a game of roller derby, each with a specific role.

This includes an alternate referee which will come into play in case of injury.

Referees primary concern is safety and ensuring the game runs smoothly, not giving out penalties.

The Jam Refs:

There are two jam referees who keep track of a jammer each, declaring lead and how many points they scored. They are also the ones who will communicate if the jammer has called the jam off.

The Inside Pack Refs (IPRs):

There are two inside pack referees, one to the front and one to the rear of the pack. Their main job is to determine where the game can take place by defining a pack. Without a pack, there is no roller derby! They tell players if they have left the active play area or if they are destroying it. These refs also look for possible penalties.

Pack is here!

The Outside Pack Refs (OPRs):

These are up to three referees skating on the outside of the track, looking for penalties and helping the other referees with anything they might not be able to see from the inside. They are the eyes on the outside of the track.

Referees skate the entire duration of the game and OPRs always skate the longest way around the track.

The Non-Skating Officials (NSOs)

The non-skating officials do a plethora of jobs to keep the game running. They tend to be asked to wear black and are never on skates. They are required for the game to run! There can be up to eleven per game.

They take care of tracking penalties and running the penalty box. They time players and send them back on track when their penalty time has expired.

They operate the scoreboard and help keep track of the score with the jam refs. They also keep a record of which player scored, when they scored and how many points they scored.

They take down game stats and keep track of penalties. There's a lot of clipboards involved!

They are the keepers of the time elapsed in each half of game, each time-out, each jam and the time between jams.

You'll see the jam timer NSO call out "five seconds" with a raised hand, wait five seconds, then lower their hand and whistle to signal the start of the jam.

What a Jam Looks Like

During each half, players will try to score points during *jams*. A jam is a segment of the game and can last up to two minutes where each team has up to five players on the track.

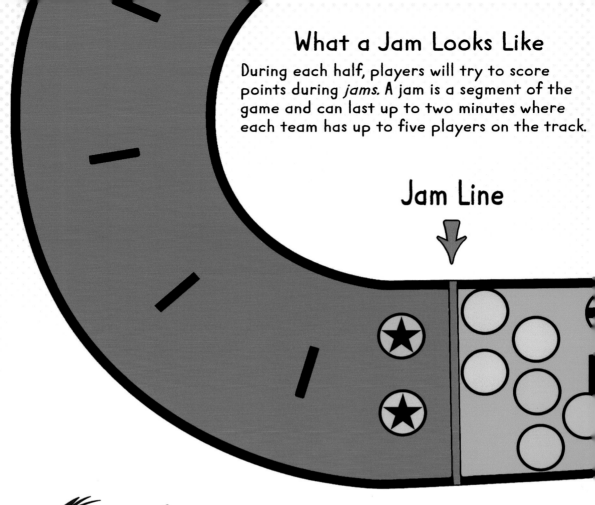

Jam Line

Jammers, the players with stars on their helmet covers, are the only ones who can score. They start each jam behind the *jam line*. This could be anywhere in the purple area above, but unless they're late getting to the track, they usually choose to start relatively close to the *jam line*.

Blockers, all the other players, start in between the *jam line* and the *pivot line*: the green area above. They cannot push, pull or interact with the opposing team until the jam-starting whistle is blown.

Each jam should start with four blockers and one jammer on each team. This includes players in the penalty box, so all players might not be on track when the starting whistle blows.

Pivot Line

Direction of play

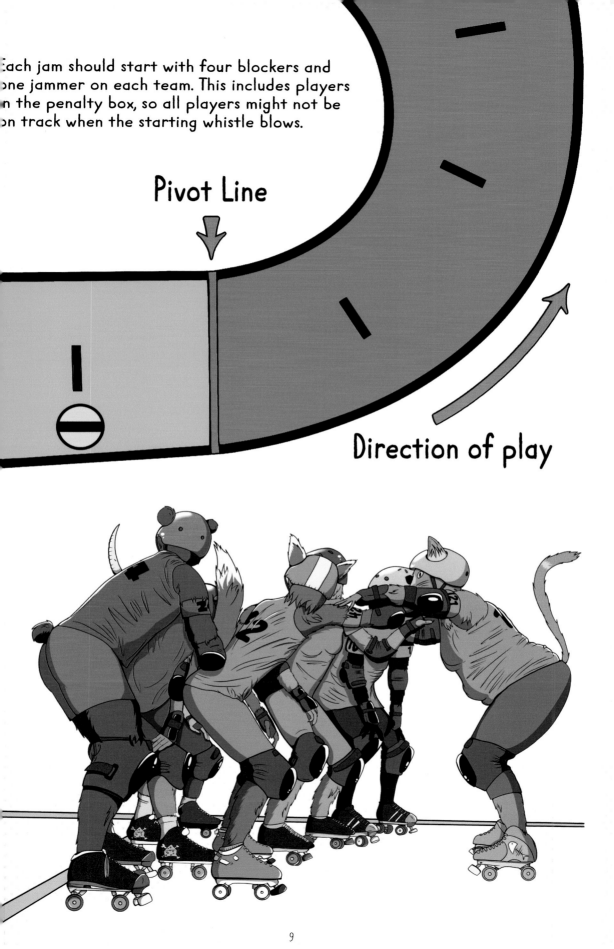

The NSO, *non-skating official*, that is close to the track, generally sporting a stopwatch and a whistle, will call "5 seconds" loudly, and indicate with their hand "5" so players can also see the warning. After 5 seconds, the NSO blows a single whistle and the jam starts.

If players move out of their designated zones before the whistle is blown, it is a *false start*, which is not a penalty, but requires the player to go behind everyone on track so they don't gain any advantage from their false start.

You might see a player with their arms up, to indicate they are not in play, skating behind the other players because they have committed a false start.

Once the jam starts, the first jammer to get ahead of all the opposing team's blockers is declared lead. That means they get the power to decide when the jam ends by calling it off. To indicate which jammer has gotten lead, a ref will blow a single whistle, point at them with one hand and make an "L" with their other hand.

The *lead jammer* can *call off the jam* by tapping their hips twice. They must make sure gesture is clear and can be seen by their jam ref. Only the jam ref assigned to them, and no other ref, can end the jam if they see this signal.

Only a lead jammer can *call off the jam*. Why would a jammer decide to do so, despite having started out of the initial pack of players first?

The main reason is to stop the other team from scoring points!

If they are overtaken by the other jammer and do not want to let the other jammer risk scoring more points.

You will generally see this immediately after the lead jammer is overtaken, or before the opposing jammer enters the pack for another scoring pass.

If the jammer is tired, if they are stuck behind the opposing blockers, or if the other team has a lot of players in the penalty box, they might also decide to call the jam.

If the *lead jammer* gets pushed off track, if they fall or lose their positional advantage, they might decide to call off the jam. As long as no penalty has been called against them, the *lead jammer* can call off the jam.

The *lead jammer* can call off the jam while outside the track after having been pushed out, or even on the floor if they fell.

Scoring

Scoring is done by the jammer's hips passing blockers' hips.

Jams are split up into passes. A pass starts when the jammer enters the engagement zone and ends when they leave it. It is basically when they go around the track and enter the pack of blockers until they have passed the pack of blockers.

A jammer can only score 4 points per pass: one for every opposing blocker. If blockers are not on track because they are in the penalty box, or simply forgot to join the jam, the points they represent are scored when the jammer passes the first blocker they can score on.

At the end of each jammer's pass, their jammer referee will lift their hand up indicating how many points were scored.

Penalty Box

When a player gets a penalty, they must skate to the penalty box and stay there for 30 seconds per penalty. You will rarely see a player get more than one penalty at a time.

The penalty box is divided into two sections, one for each team:
Each team's section will have two seats for blockers, marked by a "B" and one for a jammer, marked by a "J".

When a player only has 10 seconds left in the penalty box, they will be asked to stand. This is so they will be ready to return to track and for other players on track to know they will soon be returning.

Typically, only one of the two jammers will be sitting a penalty at a time.

If a jammer enters the penalty box while another jammer is already serving a penalty, the jammer already sitting will be allowed to go back on the track while the jammer arriving will only have to serve a penalty for as long as the previous jammer sat in the penalty box.

This keeps the game from stopping. If both jammers are in the penalty box, then nothing is going on track.

If any jammer gets sent to the penalty box, the jam becomes a *power jam* until the jammer leaves the penalty box or the jammer on track is sent to the penalty box.

During a *power jam,* only one team can score, giving them a big advantage!

If a lead jammer is sent to the penalty box, they lose the ability to call it off!

If that happens, and there is no lead jammer, then the jam goes on for two minutes and gets called by the jam timer.

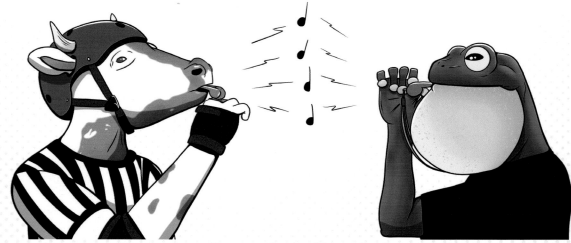

When the jam ends, whether if was called off by the lead jammer, or it reached its maximum length of two minutes, the ref or jam timer will blow four short consecutive whistles, which is then echoed by the rest of the refs, just to make sure everyone is aware the jam has ended.

Penalties

The game of roller derby is about scoring points in order to win. This has to be done while following rules, created with the *safety* of players in mind above all else. Refs are in charge of enforcing the rules on track and will give penalties to players, sending them to the penalty box, when they break them.

If a player accumulates 7 penalties they will *foul out* of the game and be asked to leave the game and join the spectators.

Refs can also eject players from the game or venue if the deem the skater unsafe on the track, have caused or tried to cause intentional harm to others, or have been showing disrespect towards officials or other players, including their own team-mates.

Only one penalty will be given per fouling instance. If a player does a back block with their forearms, for example, they will only get one penalty.

Refs and more rarely NSOs will give penalties by:

1 - Blowing a single whistle

2 - Calling the offending player's team colour, then number

3 - Announcing the penalty, accompanied with a hand signal

Pack Rules

The *pack* is what defines where the contact, scoring and game can take place on the track. The pack is defined by the largest group of blockers containing players from both teams within 10 feet/3 metres of each other. It must contain players from both teams! Defining the *pack* is a key role of *inside pack refs*.

The *engagement zone*, where contact can happen, is defined by the location of the *pack*. The engagement zone extends 20 feet/6 metres in front of the foremost skater of the *pack* and behind the rearmost skater of the pack.

Players outside the engagement zone will be told by refs they are out of play and will need to return to the engagement zone or get a penalty.

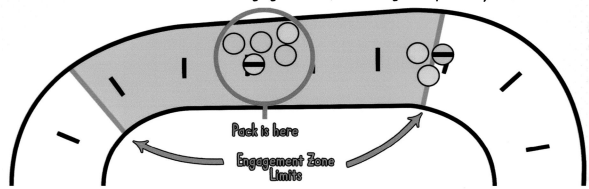

You might see players trying to make the pack as wide as possible in order to expand the engagement zone. This is generally to allow them to legally block opponents further down the track.

Players might extend their arms to help them judge how far they are from each other when they want to stretch the pack.

To signal there is no pack, the rear or front inside pack ref will put their arms in the air yelling "no pack" and keep them there until a pack is reformed. They will then signal where the pack is with their arms yelling "pack is here".

Destruction of pack:

A player will be given a *destruction of pack* penalty if they move so that there is no defined pack on track and fail to get back into position to reform the pack.

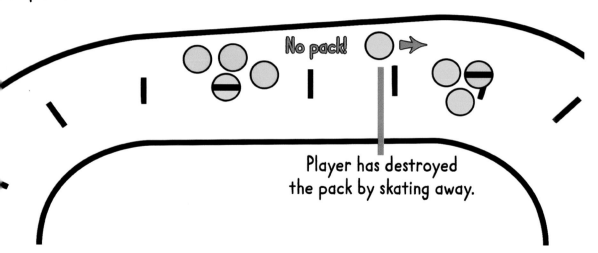

Player has destroyed the pack by skating away.

Failure to reform:

If there is no pack, blockers from both teams must actively work to reform it. Failing to do so will bring forward a *failure to reform* penalty.

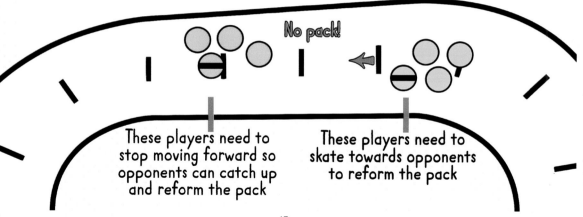

These players need to stop moving forward so opponents can catch up and reform the pack

These players need to skate towards opponents to reform the pack

Direction and Stop Blocks

When a player blocks another, they must still follow the direction of play also known as *derby-direction*. They are not allowed to stop a player from going forward completely and can only slow them down. Stopping a player completely is called a *stop block*.

Players are not allowed to push opponents in anti-derby direction – against the direction of play. This is a penalty called *direction*.

The blocking skater is moving in *derby-direction,* this is legal.

The blocking skater is not moving and stopping the opponent from moving. This is a *stop-block*.

The blocking skater is pushing the opponent against the direction of play. This is a *direction* penalty.

Cut track

If a skater goes off the track, they must re-enter the track behind everyone else that was in front of them when this happened or the skater that pushed them off and behind skaters that were in front of them when they were pushed off track.

Here the orange skater gets pushed off track by the pink skater.

The orange skater re-enters the track in front of the pink skater, who pushed them off.

The orange skater will be issued a cut track penalty. They should have re-entered the track behind the pink skater.

It is important to note players have a chance to correct this before being assessed a penalty. They can come back off the track and re-enter legally. This is one of the few penalties that can be corrected. This was implemented to keep the game flowing as much as possible.

A cut is a relatively common penalty. The ref hand signal for this is making a cross with their arms in the air.

Recycling

Recycling is a very common tactic born from the *cut track* rule. It is a strategy and not mentioned in the rules.

If a skater goes off the track accidentally, they must re-enter behind everyone that was in front of them when they left the track. Skaters in front of them will *skate anti-derby direction* to force the player to re-enter further back than where they left track.

Blue skater is pushed off the track

You will see a player go off track and skaters from the opposing team skating backwards to make them lose progression. Because of the direction rule, the players cannot make contact with opponents when recycling another player.

A skater will knock an opposing player, generally the jammer, off track and skate back, against the direction of play and the opposing player that was pushed off has to re-enter behind the skater that pushed them out and will lose progression.

Red skater starts going against the direction of play so blue skater will lose progress.

Blue skater must reenter the track behind the red skater in order to avoid a *cut track penalty.*

Star Pass

The jammer is allowed to give the pivot the star helmet cover as long as they are both upright and inbounds.

Once the pivot puts on the helmet cover, they become the jammer and can score points.

The star helmet cover must be worn in order to score points!

Only the jammer and pivot are allowed to touch the star helmet cover. Anyone else touching it will incur a penalty.

If a jammer with lead removes their star, they will lose lead jammer status.

If no lead jammer has been declared and a jammer removes their star, they lose the ability to become lead!

Walls

The classic derby defence is to create walls. This is where two or more blockers work together to stop opposing skaters.

The three-wall is when two blockers present their backs to the opposing skaters while being guided and stabilised by a third skater bracing them. In walls, presenting your back to block a skater is the preferred strategy as it offers less legal contact areas, limiting the areas that an opponent can make contact with.

When forming walls, players cannot form unbreakable links, like locking arms. Doing this is called a *multiplayer block*. This is generally defined by a link, that if challenged, could not be broken without causing injury to a player. Safety is always at the forefront of rules!

Here we have two players locking arms to block an opponent. The opponent could not break through without breaking their arms. This is a common *multiplayer block*.

Some players prefer using a wall formed of only two players. It can also come into action team-mates are in the penalty box or separated on the track.

Even with two players, blockers have to be careful they do not create a *multiplayer block*, like by holding onto one another. If a hold is challenged by an opposing player, the blockers will have to let it go. If they hold back an opponent with a such a link, it is also a *multiplayer block*.

One on one blocking is also used and can be a very useful measure to give time for the rest of the blockers to reset themselves and form a stronger wall ahead.

Apex Jump

One of the most impressive roller derby jammer moves is the apex jump. The jammer will jump over the apex of the track passing the other team's blockers to score. It's difficult to pull off though!

For this to succeed, they must take off inbounds and land inbounds and upright without hitting other blockers. If they hit a blocker, it might be *leaping contact* which is a penalty. It can also lead to serious injury.

Offence

Blockers can play offensively to help their jammer score, instead of defensively to stop the opposing jammer from scoring. Generally, the pivot blocker will do the most offence for their jammer as being near the jammer allows them to receive a star pass easily.

There are many offensive strategies. You might see a player disrupting the opposing players' attempts to form a wall, or even breaking up already formed walls.

Here, for example, the blue pivot pushed the opponents out of the way of the blue jammer to allow them to pass more easily.

Time Out and Official Review

Each team is allowed 3 x 1 minute *time outs* per game which can be taken between jams.

These are tracked on the scoreboard.

Each team is allowed 1 *official review* per gamehalf. With this, they can question an official's decision from the previous jam.

Team Time Out

Official Review

During the official review, the refs will discuss the decision the captains want to review from the previous jam.

The captains will explain to the officials what decision they would like to contest.

The officials will discuss their previous assessment amongst themselves and might go back on their previous decision.

If the captains are successful in the challenge of the refs' past decision, it will be corrected as best as can be. This might be done by changing the score or removing a penalty.

If the official review passes, the team will retain their official review and can use it one more time. If they are not, they lose it.

Teams can also use the official review as an additional timeout.

Official Time Out

What parts of the body can be targeted by blocks

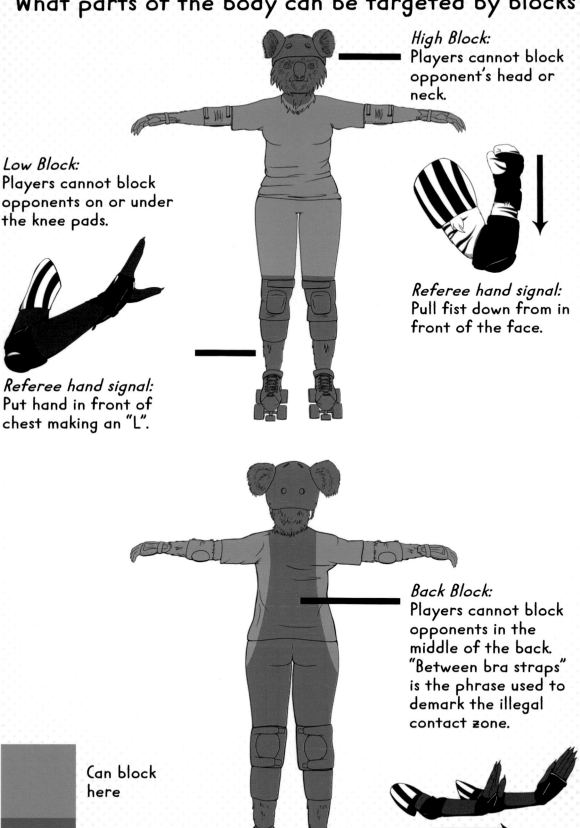

High Block:
Players cannot block opponent's head or neck.

Referee hand signal:
Pull fist down from in front of the face.

Low Block:
Players cannot block opponents on or under the knee pads.

Referee hand signal:
Put hand in front of chest making an "L".

Back Block:
Players cannot block opponents in the middle of the back. "Between bra straps" is the phrase used to demark the illegal contact zone.

Referee hand signal:
Pushing both hands forward.

Can block here

Cannot block here

What parts of the body can be used to block

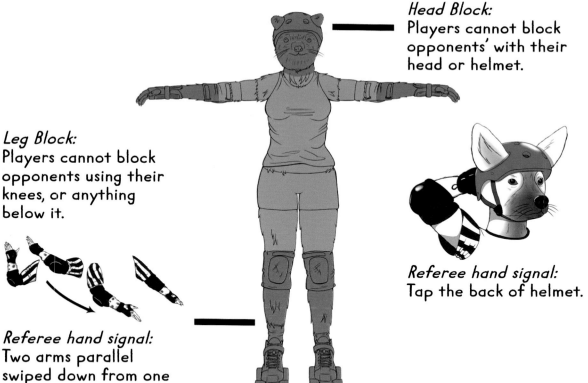

Head Block:
Players cannot block opponents' with their head or helmet.

Referee hand signal:
Tap the back of helmet.

Leg Block:
Players cannot block opponents using their knees, or anything below it.

Referee hand signal:
Two arms parallel swiped down from one side to the other.

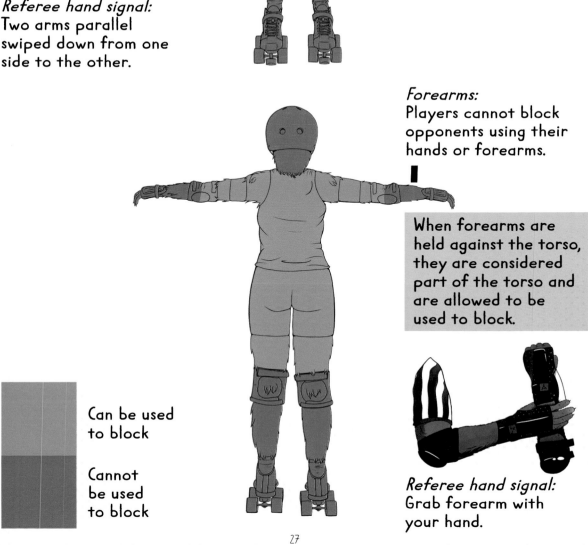

Forearms:
Players cannot block opponents using their hands or forearms.

When forearms are held against the torso, they are considered part of the torso and are allowed to be used to block.

Referee hand signal:
Grab forearm with your hand.

Can be used to block

Cannot be used to block

Common Penalty Hand Signals

Direction and *Stop Block:*
While blocking, players cannot push opponents against the direction of play (*direction*) nor hold a player in place (*stop block*).

Referee hand signal: Move arm from one side to another.

Multiplayer Block:
Players cannot stop the other team by forming an impenetrable wall by grabbing each other. They can lean or rest on each other, but if they lock onto one-another, that is a *multiplayer block penalty.*

Referee hand signal: Clasp fingers from each hand together.

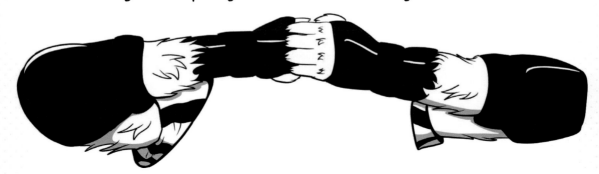

Cut Track Penalty:
Players cannot re-enter the track in front of those who knocked them off.

Referee hand signal: Cross forearms.

Interference:
Players cannot delay the game, like by having the wrong number of players on track.

Referee hand signal: Brush down arm

Out of Play and Illegal Position:

Players must stay within the engagement zone or they will be told they are out of play. Failing to return to the engagement zone is an *illegal position penalty*. An *out of play* warning is generally given before assessing the penalty.

Referee hand signal: lift one arm for *out of play* and lower it in a chopping motion for *illegal position.*

Illegal Contact:

Players engaging in a block outside of the engagement zone are given an *illegal contact penalty.*

Referee hand signal: make a chopping motion with one hand into the other.

Illegal Procedure:

Players cannot break the rules of a star pass or other procedures.

Referee hand signal: spin forearms around each other.

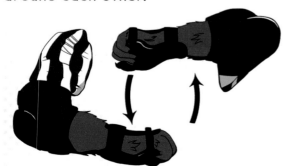

Misconduct:

Players cannot misbehave towards officials and other players.

Referee hand signal: drag hand in front of the neck.

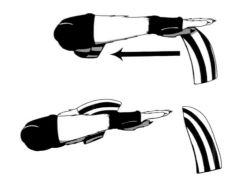

How to Read the Scoreboard

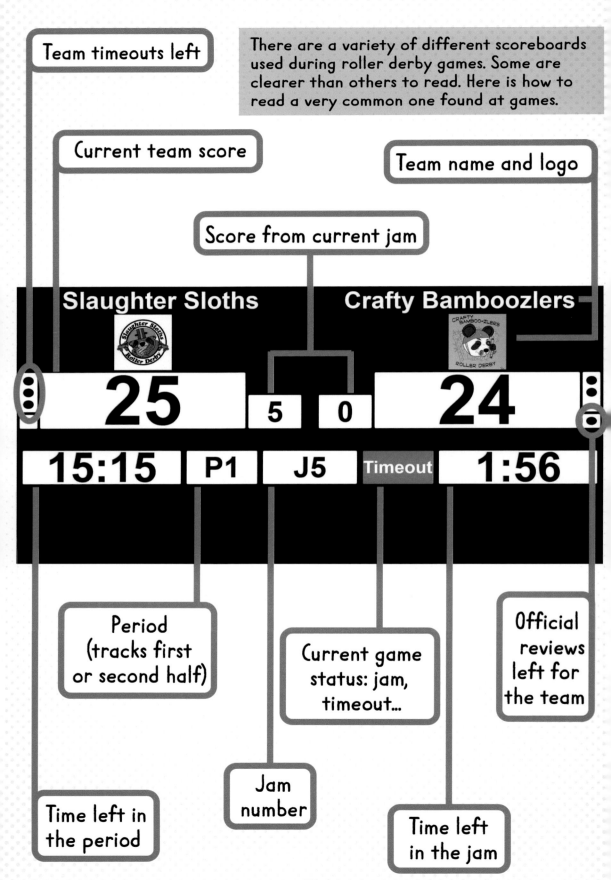

There are a variety of different scoreboards used during roller derby games. Some are clearer than others to read. Here is how to read a very common one found at games.

Team timeouts left

Current team score

Team name and logo

Score from current jam

Slaughter Sloths

Crafty Bamboozlers

25 5 0 **24**

15:15 P1 J5 Timeout **1:56**

Period (tracks first or second half)

Current game status: jam, timeout...

Official reviews left for the team

Time left in the period

Jam number

Time left in the jam

30

Glossary

Alternate	Player or bench crew alternate to the captain. They can also weigh in during official reviews.
Alternate Referee/Alt	Referee who is off skates, generally near the penalty box. They will observe but their main role is to replace a skating referee in case of injury.
Blocker	Skater which is not the jammer. They cannot score points.
Calling Off a Jam/Calling It	Action the lead jammer can take by hitting their hips twice to end the jam.
Captain	Skater who can talk to referees during official reviews. They will also sit for penalties allocated to the team or a skater who cannot sit themself.
Engagement Zone	Area of the track where skaters can engage in contact and blocking opposing players.
Foul Out	After accumulating seven penalties, a player will foul out, not being able to return to track and asked to join the specatators.
Head Referee/HR	The referee in charge of other referees. They have the final say on decisions taken by officials.
Inside Pack Referee/IPR	Referees located on the inside of the track whose role is mainly to define the pack and therefore the engagement zone.
Jam	A segment of the game which can last up to two minutes.
Jam Line	Line on the track where jammers have to start behind and blockers in front of.
Jam Referee/JR	Referee in charge of a specific jammer whose main role is to count the points scored by their jammer.
Jam Timer/JT	Official in charge of timing the game and jams who will announce when jams are about to start then whistle the beginning of a jam.

Jammer	Skater with a star on their helmet cover who can score points by passing the hips of opposing blockers.
Lead Jammer	Jammer who has passed the pack first during the initial pass of the jam.
Lineup Tracker/LT	Official who tracks which players are participating in each jam, making sure no injured players are on track.
Non-Skating Official/NSO	Officials who are off-skates and help the game of roller derby run.
Official	On and off skate people who make help run the game of roller derby whose primary role is everyone's safety.
Official Review	Opportunity for a team to contest a decision by officials. It can be retained once if the official review is succesful. Each team starts with one.
Official Timeout	Timeout requested by officials if they need more than the 30 seconds between jams to enssure the game continues smoothly.
Outside Pack Referee/OPR	Referees located on the outside of the track who gain a different view of the game.
Pack	The largest group of blockers on track made up of skaters from both teams.
Penalty	An infraction of the rules by a skater which leads them to spend 30 seconds sat in the penalty box. Seven penailties will lead to a skater fouling out.
Penalty Box	Area with chairs where players will have to sit to serve their penalty time.
Penalty Box Manager/PBM	Official who manages the penalty box and makes sure jammers are swapped out from the box appropriately.
Penalty Box Operator/PBO	Official timing the players in the penalty box, telling them where to sit, when to stand and when to return to track.

Pentalty Tracker/PT	Official who tracks penalties, making sure players who have accumulated seven penalties get fouled out.
Period/Half	Half of the game, normally 30 minutes.
Pivot Blocker	Blocker who can claim the pivot line and receive a star pass as well as legally touch the star helmet cover, if it falls for example.
Pivot Line	The line blockers have to start behind and jammers in front. If claimed by a pivot, blockers must start behind the pivot's hips.
Referee/Ref	Skating official whose primary concern is safety. They also count points and give penalties.
Scoreboard Operator/SBO	Official who operates the scoreboard during the game, communicating with other officials to make sure the information displayed is accurate.
Star Pass	When the jammer passes the star helmet cover to their team's pivot blocker.
Team Timeout	Timeout requested by teams. Each team has three per game. They last one minute each.
Volunteer	Volunteers include officials as well as people helping the game run smoothly, such as track maintenance.
Wall	Group of blockers working together to stop an opposing jammer.

Now that you're a derby expert, want to get involved?

The Women's Flat Track Derby Assocation is the international governing body of roller derby and is democratically run by its member leagues.

The WFTDA sets the international standards for:

Rankings and Competition

Rules and Gameplay

Safety and Regulations

Check out wftda.com to:
- Find WFTDA member leagues in your area
- Become a WFTDA member league
- Discover upcoming events
- Donate to the WFTDA or find out more about partnership opportunities
- AND MORE!

Follow the WFTDA on: